Prostate Cancer UK is a registered charity in England and Wales (1005541) and in Scotland (SC039332).
Registered company 02653887.

For uncles and brothers,
for sons and for friends,
for fathers and families,
for the love that never ends.

For carers and healers,
the researchers too,
and for my dad, my hero,
this moon is for you.

The Man Who Hung the Moon

Author G.L. Stone
Illustrator Elina Oplakanska

This is the tale my father once told,
Of far-off adventures where wonders unfold.
Tales of a bright silvery moon,
Hung by a man with a red balloon.

Each night he'd float with it tied to his back,
And pull out the moon from inside his sack.
He'd whistle a tune as he sewed it in place,
With stitches of starlight gathered from space.

He polished it gently till it gleamed with a grin,
Then drifted in silence as night settled in.

He watched through the stillness, the stars all aglow,
Guarding the moon from the mischief below.

One night, sailing, from behind the sun-
Pirates! To snatch what he'd only just hung!
They rattled their chains and they bellowed with glee,
'The moon be ours — for the scurvy crew an' me!'

"**Never!**" he steered his red balloon high,
BANG went the cannons that lit up the sky!
He flung fiery stars that spun all around,
As the ship wobbled sideways, then flipped upside down!
"Retreat!" cried the Captain, his crew took to flight,
As they tumbled away and vanished from sight.

The man floated back, as he gently swayed,
He heard the cries of the moon-mouse parade!
With squeaks and squeals, the mice made their pleas,
Chanting and cheering, 'Give us the moon cheese!"

"**Never!**" he steered his red balloon high,
As mice on bright bubbles bounced through the sky.
He took a deep breath, no time to delay,
And with one big puff, he blew them away!
"Retreat!" squeaked a moonmouse, clutching on tight,
As they tumbled away and vanished from sight.

The man floated back, drifting through the night,
When Martians on meteors rode into sight!
"Give us the moon! Its glow we must take,
To splash on our mountains and shine on our lakes."

"**Never!**" he steered his red balloon high,
As they reached for the moonlight, way up in the sky.
He drew his star-string racket with flick and with flair,
He sent the Martians cartwheeling, right through the air!
"Retreat!" cried the Martians, as they clung on tight,
Bouncing and bobbing, as they vanished from sight.

As skies grew calm, he watched from above,
Guarding his world with endless love.

On quiet nights, he would settle just so,
Sitting on the moon, singing soft and low:
"While you sleep and the night winds blow,
I'll guard your magic and watch it grow."

With dreams all stitched, his missions complete,
He drifted down to the moon's starlit seat.
There he rested, where silver light kissed,
And the night held him gently in cosmic mist.

This was the tale my father once told,
Of far-off adventures as the years grew old.
Tales of a balloon he'd one day give me,
To hang up the moon for all to see.

I'd ride silver whales through the inky night sky,
And chase away monsters that tiptoed nearby.
I'd hang it to glow, in the silence of space,
A little like him, stitching a dream in place.

Copyright © G.L.Stone 2025

Author: G.L.Stone
Artwork: Elina Oplakanska

Title: The Man Who Hung the Moon

All rights reserved. No part of this book may be reproduced or used in any manner without the prior written permission of the copyright owner.

www.ingramcontent.com/pod-product-compliance
Lightning Source LLC
Chambersburg PA
CBHW041125070526
44584CB00003B/279